Lerner SPORTS

SPORTS TEAM SMACKDOWN

KANSAS CITY CHIEFS VS. LAS VEGAS RAIDERS

RIVAL RUMBLE

ABBY COLICH

Lerner Publications ◆ Minneapolis

Stats in this book are accurate through the 2025 Super Bowl.

Lerner Publications Company
An imprint of Lerner Publishing Group, Inc.
241 First Avenue North
Minneapolis, MN 55401 USA

For reading levels and more information, look up this title at www.lernerbooks.com.

Main body text set in Aptifer Sans LT Pro.
Typeface provided by Linotype AG.

Editor: Matt Doeden

Library of Congress Cataloging-in-Publication Data

Names: Colich, Abby, author.
Title: Kansas City Chiefs vs. Las Vegas Raiders : rival rumble / Abby Colich.
Other titles: Kansas City Chiefs versus Las Vegas Raiders
Description: Minneapolis : Lerner Publications, 2026. | Series: Lerner sports. Sports team smackdown | Includes bibliographical references and index. | Audience: Ages 7–11 | Audience: Grades 4–6 | Summary: "With seven total Super Bowl wins, the Kansas City Chiefs and Las Vegas Raiders both have plenty to brag about. But which NFL team is better? Explore their stats and triumphs and make your decision"— Provided by publisher.
Identifiers: LCCN 2024047350 (print) | LCCN 2024047351 (ebook) | ISBN 9798765668641 (library binding) | ISBN 9798765683507 (paperback) | ISBN 9798765681619 (epub)
Subjects: LCSH: Kansas City Chiefs (Football team)—Juvenile literature. | Las Vegas Raiders (Football team)—Juvenile literature. | Sports rivalries—Juvenile literature.
Classification: LCC GV956.K35 C654 2026 (print) | LCC GV956.K35 (ebook) | DDC 796.332/6409778411—dc23/eng/20250108

LC record available at https://lccn.loc.gov/2024047350
LC ebook record available at https://lccn.loc.gov/2024047351

Manufactured in the United States of America
1-1011974-53832-3/12/2025

TABLE OF CONTENTS

INTRODUCTION

A WILD RIVALRY

The Oakland Raiders had lost four games in a row. On October 19, 2017, they played at home against their rivals, the Kansas City Chiefs.

The Raiders trailed in the fourth quarter 30–24. They had the ball at the 29-yard line with 23 seconds to go. On third down, quarterback Derek Carr passed to tight end Jared Cook. Cook caught the ball as he rolled into the end zone.

Tyreek Hill hauls in a touchdown pass to help the Chiefs build a lead over the Raiders in 2017.

At first, the refs called it a touchdown. But after watching the replay, they reversed the call. Cook had actually caught the ball just short of the end zone.

The game clock ticked down to eight seconds. Carr passed the ball to wide receiver Michael Crabtree in the end zone. But the refs took away the touchdown after a Raiders penalty.

After two penalties on the Chiefs, the Raiders had the ball with time for one more play. Carr dropped back and saw Crabtree open. Carr zipped a pass to the wide receiver, who caught it for

FAST FACTS

- The Chiefs and Raiders were in the American Football League and joined the NFL in 1970.
- The Raiders played in Oakland and Los Angeles, California, before moving to Las Vegas, Nevada, in 2020.
- Chiefs linebacker Derrick Thomas holds the NFL record for most sacks in a game with seven.
- The Raiders scored a team record 42 points in the first half of a 2023 game against the Los Angeles Chargers. The Raiders went on to win 63-21.

the score. The Raiders kicked the extra point to win 31–30. The game was called the Thursday Night Thriller. It was a wild game in the long rivalry between the teams.

Michael Crabtree and teammates celebrate their last-minute touchdown to beat the Chiefs.

SMACKDOWN!

CHAPTER 1

Quarterback Len Dawson (number 16) calls the next play during the 1970 Super Bowl against the Minnesota Vikings.

TWO TOUGH TEAMS

Both the Chiefs and the Raiders formed in 1960 as part of the newly created American Football League (AFL). The Chiefs started out as the Dallas Texans. In 1962, they were the AFL champs. A year later, they moved to Kansas City, Missouri, and changed their name to the Chiefs. In 1967, they played in the first Super Bowl but lost to the Green Bay Packers 35–10. Three years later, the Chiefs returned to the Super Bowl and beat the Minnesota Vikings.

The Chiefs joined the National Football League (NFL) in 1970. They won their division in 1971 but didn't make it to the playoffs again until 1986.

In 2013, the Chiefs hired head coach Andy Reid. The team drafted quarterback Patrick Mahomes in 2017. Together, Reid and Mahomes have helped create one of the NFL's top teams, winning Super Bowls in 2020, 2023, and 2024.

Andy Reid has been one of the NFL's most successful head coaches with the Chiefs.

The Raiders played in Oakland from 1960 to 1981. During this time, they were known for their toughness. They won an AFL Championship in 1967 and Super Bowls in 1977 and 1981.

The Raiders moved to Los Angeles in 1982. They beat Washington in the Super Bowl in 1984 and won their division in 1991. But they did not have any other playoff success during their time in Los Angeles.

Marcus Allen (left) celebrates the Raiders Super Bowl win with a teammate in 1984.

Raiders players run off the field after an overtime victory in 2022.

The Raiders moved back to Oakland in 1995. They played in the Super Bowl in 2003 but lost to the Tampa Bay Buccaneers 48–21. Since that loss in the Super Bowl, they have only made it to the playoffs two times.

In 2020, the Raiders moved to Las Vegas. They play home games in a brand-new stadium that holds 65,000 fans.

The rivalry between the Chiefs and Raiders goes back to when both teams played in the AFL. The Raiders lost the rivals' first meeting in 1960. But they came back to win by a point when they met again a few weeks later.

The teams have met three times in the playoffs. In 1968, they battled in the first round. The Raiders came out on top, winning 41–6. The next season, the teams met in the AFL Championship Game with a trip to the Super Bowl on the line. The Chiefs won 17–7 and went on to win the Super Bowl.

Len Dawson (right) drops back as the Kansas City offensive line blocks in front of him.

Raiders wide receiver Fred Biletnikoff runs after catching a pass while Kansas City defender Goldie Sellers makes the tackle.

Since then, the teams have taken turns dominating their division. The Raiders ruled in the 1970s. The Chiefs have owned recent decades.

CHECK IT OUT

From 1969 to 1978, John Madden led the Raiders to 103 wins, more than any other Raiders head coach. After coaching, he was an NFL commentator for 30 years. He also helped create the Madden NFL video game series.

CHAPTER 2

Otis Taylor (top) is tackled during the 1970 Super Bowl.

MOST THRILLING MOMENTS

Fans of both the Chiefs and the Raiders have seen some exciting games from their teams. The Chiefs went into the 1970 Super Bowl as underdogs. But wide receiver Otis Taylor helped lead the team to a surprising win over the Minnesota Vikings, dominating them for a final score of 23–7. Taylor caught six passes, including a 46-yard touchdown in the third quarter.

When the 2015 season ended, the Chiefs hadn't won a playoff game in nearly 22 years. But going into a first-round matchup against the Houston Texans, they were determined to end this losing streak. Knile Davis opened the game with a 106-yard kickoff return for a touchdown. Quarterback Alex Smith led the Chiefs offense completing 17 of 22 passes. The defense forced five turnovers to keep the Texans scoreless. The Chiefs won 30–0.

Quarterback Alex Smith looks for a receiver in the Chiefs 30–0 playoff victory over the Texans.

Quarterback Patrick Mahomes (left) is under pressure from San Francisco 49ers defensive end Nick Bosa in the 2024 Super Bowl.

The Chiefs returned to the Super Bowl in 2024. They trailed the San Francisco 49ers 19–16 in the fourth quarter. With three seconds left, the Chiefs kicked a field goal to tie. Then, in overtime, quarterback Patrick Mahomes passed the ball to wide receiver Mecole Hardman for a touchdown. The Chiefs won their second Super Bowl in a row.

CHECK IT OUT

Chiefs fans hold the record as the loudest fans. In 2014, the crowd reached 142.2 decibels. That's as loud as standing at one end of a football field and hearing a jet take off from the other side.

The Raiders have had plenty of their own great moments. In a December 21, 1974, playoff game, the Raiders were down 26–21 against the Miami Dolphins. With less than a minute to go, quarterback Ken Stabler threw a desperate pass into a crowd of players. Luckily, running back Clarence Davis came away with the ball. The Raiders scored and won the game.

During a game on December 18, 2016, with 2:40 left on the game clock, Sebastian Janikowski kicked a field goal to beat the San Diego Chargers. The win sent the Raiders to the playoffs for the first time since 2002.

Quarterback Ken Stabler hurls a pass in the Raiders playoff win over the Dolphins in 1974.

Wide receiver Davante Adams hauls in a touchdown catch for the Raiders in 2023.

The Raiders suffered a low in December 2023. They didn't score a single point in a game against the Vikings. But the next week, they came back with a high. They outscored the Los Angeles Chargers 42–0 in the first half of the game. That was a team record for the most points in a first half. The Raiders went on to win 63–21.

The Chiefs and Raiders have had many close games against each other. On January 2, 2000, the Chiefs were one win away from making it to the playoffs. With 45 seconds to go, the Raiders scored a field goal to send the game into overtime. A few minutes later, another field goal won the game for the Raiders, knocking the Chiefs out of the playoffs.

On November 6, 2005, the Chiefs were down 23–20 to the Raiders with five seconds remaining. The Chiefs had the ball five yards from the end zone. Instead of going for a field goal to tie and send the game into overtime, they went for the touchdown. Larry Johnson ran the ball into the end zone for the win.

On December 25, 2023, the Raiders came to Kansas City as underdogs. In the second quarter, the Raiders scored on a Chiefs fumble and again on an interception. The Chiefs couldn't recover from their mistakes. The Raiders won 20–14.

Kansas City running back Isiah Pacheco loses his helmet as Raiders players tackle him in this 2023 game.

CHAPTER 3

Len Dawson throws the ball for the Chiefs in the first Super Bowl on January 15, 1967.

GREAT PLAYERS

Some of the NFL's greatest have played for the Chiefs and Raiders. Len Dawson was the Chiefs quarterback from 1962 to 1975. He led the team to their first Super Bowl title in 1970.

Receiver Otis Taylor was one of Dawson's favorite targets. He held many team receiving records during his time as a player from 1965 to 1975.

Willie Lanier played for the Chiefs from 1967 to 1977. The linebacker had 27 career interceptions. He recovered 18 fumbles.

Linebacker Derrick Thomas played for the Chiefs from 1989 to 1999. He had the most sacks in the NFL during that time. He still holds the NFL record for most sacks in a game with seven.

Linebacker Derrick Thomas was a fierce pass rusher and a strong tackler.

Travis Kelce (left) is Kansas City's all-time leader in receiving yards and touchdowns.

Tony Gonzalez was a Chiefs tight end from 1997 to 2008. He held many NFL records, including most career catches and most receiving yards. In 2024, Travis Kelce passed Gonzalez's team record for most receptions.

Patrick Mahomes joined the Chiefs as a quarterback in 2017. He quickly began breaking NFL records. In 2023, he became the fastest NFL player to reach 25,000 passing yards.

Many greats have played for the Raiders as well. Center Jim Otto played for the team from 1960 to 1974. He helped the Raiders win seven division championships and the 1967 AFL Championship.

Running back Marcus Allen slices through the defense with the ball in this 1985 game.

Gene Upshaw played 307 games for the team from 1967 to 1981. The offensive lineman was the first player to go to Super Bowls in three different decades.

The Raiders have had many great offensive stars. Running back Marcus Allen played for the Raiders from 1982 to 1992 and then for the Chiefs from 1993 to 1997. When he retired, he was the NFL's all-time rushing touchdown leader.

CHECK IT OUT

The Chiefs and Raiders matched up in Las Vegas for the first time in 2020. Patrick Mahomes led a touchdown drive in the final minute to give Kansas City the win.

Wide receiver Tim Brown played for the Raiders from 1988 to 2003. He holds the all-time receiving record for the team.

On defense, Charles Woodson was a Raiders safety from 1998 to 2005 and again from 2013 to 2015. His 65 career interceptions are the fifth most in NFL history.

Maxx Crosby has played for the Raiders since 2019 and is one of the NFL's top pass rushers. He ended the 2023 season with 14.5 sacks and 94 quarterback pressures.

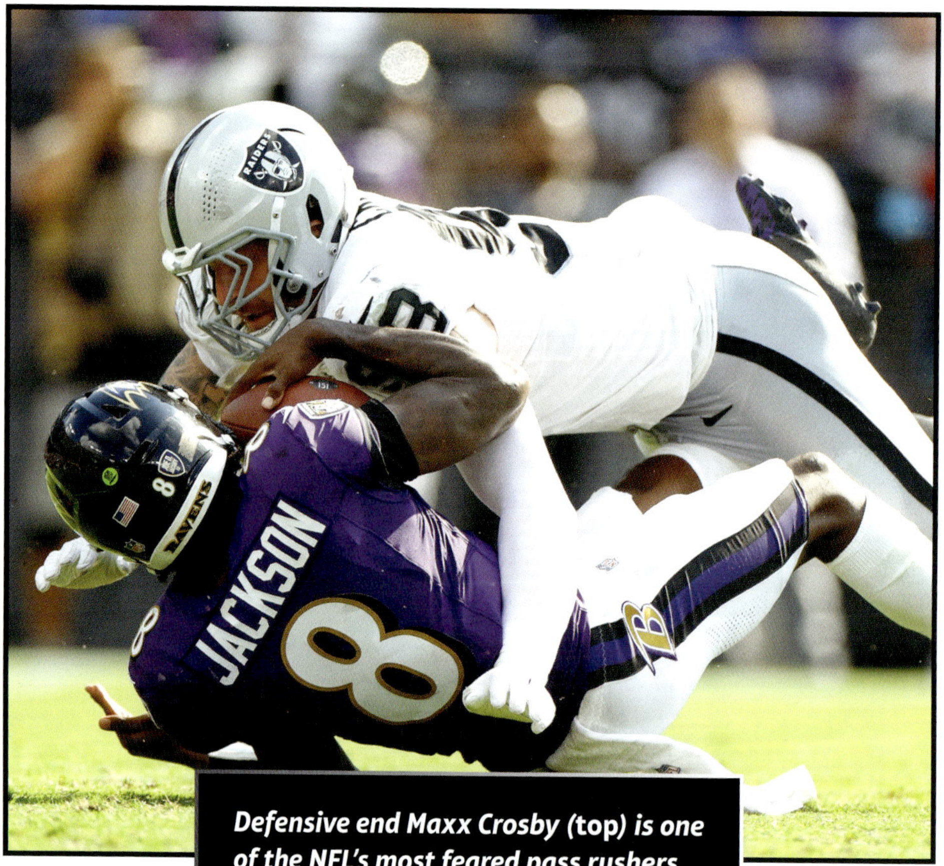

Defensive end Maxx Crosby (top) is one of the NFL's most feared pass rushers.

CHAPTER 4

Raiders quarterback Aidan O'Connell gets ready to pass the ball in a 2024 game against the Pittsburgh Steelers.

CHOOSE YOUR CHAMPION

Do you ever compare your favorite team against their top rival? Deciding which team comes out on top is one way to keep sports fun and interesting.

The Chiefs are slightly ahead when it comes to winning. They have won about 55 percent of their games all-time. The Raiders have won about 52 percent of their games.

Each team has won about the same amount of playoff games. The Raiders and Chiefs have both won four Super Bowls. But the Chiefs have won more of the matchups between the two teams.

It's a close call, but the Chiefs win this rival rumble. Which team do you choose?

It's always a battle when the Raiders and Chiefs meet on the field.

Between 2020 and 2025, Patrick Mahomes led the Chiefs to five Super Bowls.

SMACKDOWN TIMELINE

KANSAS CITY CHIEFS

1960 The Texans form in Dallas, Texas.

1963 The Texans move to Kansas City and change their name to the Chiefs.

1967 The Chiefs play in the first ever Super Bowl but lose to the Green Bay Packers.

1970 The Chiefs join the NFL.

The Chiefs beat the Minnesota Vikings to win their first Super Bowl.

2020 The Chiefs win the Super Bowl against the San Francisco 49ers.

2021 The Chiefs lose the Super Bowl to the Tampa Bay Buccaneers.

2023 The Chiefs beat the Philadelphia Eagles in the Super Bowl.

2024 The Chiefs win the Super Bowl against the San Francisco 49ers.

2025 The Chiefs lose the Super Bowl to the Philadelphia Eagles.

LAS VEGAS RAIDERS

1960 The Raiders form in Oakland, California.

1970 The Raiders join the NFL.

1977 The Raiders win the Super Bowl against the Minnesota Vikings.

1981 The Raiders beat the Philadelphia Eagles in the Super Bowl.

1982 The Raiders move to Los Angeles.

1984 The Raiders win the Super Bowl against Washington.

1995 The Raiders move back to Oakland.

2020 The Raiders move to Las Vegas.

2025 The Raiders hire new head coach Pete Carroll.

GLOSSARY

division: a group of teams that directly compete against one another

fumble: when a player loses hold of the ball while handling or running with it

interception: a pass caught by the defending team

linebacker: a defender who usually plays in the middle of the defense

pass rusher: a defensive player who tries to tackle the quarterback

pressure: when a defensive player gets near the quarterback, forcing the quarterback to run or throw the ball

ref: short for *referee*, an official who enforces football's rules during games

rivalry: when a player or team tries to defeat or be more successful than another

sack: when the quarterback is tackled for a loss of yards

tight end: a football player whose main jobs are to block defenders and catch passes

turnover: losing the ball to the opposing team

underdog: a team expected by most to lose a game

LEARN MORE

Flynn, Brendan. *Kansas City Chiefs*. Mendota Heights, MN: Apex Editions, 2025.

Levit, Joe. *Meet Patrick Mahomes*. Minneapolis: Lerner Publications, 2023.

Pro Football Hall of Fame: Kansas City Chiefs
https://www.profootballhof.com/teams/kansas-city-chiefs/

Pro Football Hall of Fame: Las Vegas Raiders
https://www.profootballhof.com/teams/las-vegas-raiders/

Sports Illustrated Kids: Football
https://www.sikids.com/football

Whiting, Jim. *The Story of the Las Vegas Raiders*. Mankato, MN: Creative Education, 2025.

INDEX

PHOTO ACKNOWLEDGMENTS

Image credits: Ezra Shaw/Getty Images, p. 4; Thearon W. Henderson/Getty Images, p. 6; Michael Owens via AP, p. 7 (top); Brooke Sutton via AP, p. 7 (bottom); Focus on Sport via Getty Images, pp. 8, 14, 21; Michael Hickey/Getty Images, p. 9; Bettmann/Getty Images, pp. 10, 13; Ethan Miller/Getty Images, pp. 11, 16; Rich Clarkson/Rich Clarkson Associates via AP Images, p. 12; Thomas B. Shea/Getty Images, p. 15; Michael Zagaris/Getty Images, p. 17; Michael Owens/Getty Images, pp. 18, 27; Jamie Squire/Getty Images, p. 19; James Flores/Getty Images, p. 20; David Eulitt/Getty Images p. 22; Bob Riha, Jr./Getty Images, p. 23; Brandon Sloter/Getty Images, p. 24; AP Photo/David Becker, p. 25; Erick W. Rasco/Sports Illustrated via Getty Images, p. 26.

Design elements: Trisno Wardana/Shutterstock; Ihor Biliavskyi/Shutterstock; Joko Ribowo/Shutterstock.

Cover: AP Photo/Ed Zurga (top); Peter Read Miller via AP (bottom).